Teaching Young Multilingual Learners

Other Redleaf Press books by Angèle Sancho Passe

Creating Diversity-Rich Environments for Young Children

Dual-Language Learners: Strategies for Teaching English

Early Childhood Leadership and Program Management

Evaluating and Supporting Early Childhood Teachers

I'm Going to Kindergarten!

Ready for Kindergarten: A Tool Kit for Supporting Children and Families, 2nd Edition

Redleaf *Quick* Guide

Teaching Young Multilingual Learners

Angèle Sancho Passe

Published by Redleaf Press
10 Yorkton Court
St. Paul, MN 55117
www.redleafpress.org

© 2025 by Redleaf Press

All rights reserved. Unless otherwise noted on a specific page, no portion of this publication may be reproduced or transmitted in any form or by any means, electronic or mechanical, including photocopying, recording, or capturing on any information storage and retrieval system, without permission in writing from the publisher, except by a reviewer, who may quote brief passages in a critical article or review to be printed in a magazine or newspaper, or electronically transmitted on radio, television, or the internet.

First edition 2025
Cover photograph by Adobe Stock/Vane Nunes
Typeset in Signo and Avenir by Douglas Schmitz
Printed in the United States of America
32 31 30 29 28 27 26 25   1 2 3 4 5 6 7 8

Library of Congress Cataloging-in-Publication Data

Names: Passe, Angèle Sancho, author.
Title: Teaching young multilingual learners / by Angèle Sancho Passe.
Description: First edition. | St. Paul, MN : Redleaf Press, 2025. |
  Includes bibliographical references. | Summary: "Teaching in a program where multiple languages are spoken presents complexities and challenges, but being multilingual brings so many lifelong benefits to children. With practical and effective advice, this guide honors the linguistic and socio-cultural goals of language learning of all children, including children with disabilities and other support needs, by taking a diversity and equity perspective in the work of teaching and fostering positive relationships among children, families, and staff"— Provided by publisher.
Identifiers: LCCN 2025012703 (print) | LCCN 2025012704 (ebook) | ISBN 9781605548463 (paperback) | ISBN 9781605548470 (ebook)
Subjects: LCSH: Multilingual education. | Language acquisition.
Classification: LCC LC3715 .P37 2025 (print) | LCC LC3715 (ebook) | DDC 372.01/175--dc23/eng/20250528
LC record available at https://lccn.loc.gov/2025012703
LC ebook record available at https://lccn.loc.gov/2025012704

Printed on acid-free paper

To all early educators who teach young multilingual learners with care and skill.
You do more than teach language. You build a multicultural world.

CONTENTS

Acknowledgments ix

Introduction xi

Chapter 1: First and Second Language Development 1

Chapter 2: Planning Programs 7

Chapter 3: Working with Families 11

Chapter 4: Supporting Monolingual Educators 15

Chapter 5: Supporting Multilingual Educators 19

Chapter 6: The Environment, Curriculum, and Materials 23

Chapter 7: Teaching the Second Language 27

Chapter 8: Honoring Home Languages 33

Chapter 9: Assessment 37

Chapter 10: Behavior Guidance 41

Conclusion: A Multilingual, Multicultural Planet 45

Checklist 49

Resources 55

References 57

ACKNOWLEDGMENTS

I am multilingual, and everybody in my family is too, so my interest in multilingual learners is both personal and professional. In addition to the research, many formal and informal exchanges have shaped my thinking over time. The ideas in this book are not just mine. I especially want to thank my family: husband Jim, children Oliver and Alexia, grandchildren Matthew and Alexander, brother Richard, parents Ricardo and Jeanine. Thank you also to my colleagues Carolina Dufault, Hannah Riddle, Carol Will, Maureen Seiwert, Marian Hassan, Yer Vang, Susana Espinosa, Mary Mackedanz, Kate Horst, Sarah Swanson, and Kamna Seth for their insights and encouragement. And finally, my heartfelt gratitude goes to my editor at Redleaf Press, Melissa York. As an exophonic writer—one who writes in a language that is not their first—I very much appreciate Melissa's skill and grace.

INTRODUCTION

Andy's family has just arrived from Mexico. The family speaks Spanish at home, and they want him to be ready for kindergarten the next fall. In Andy's preschool program, the language of instruction is English. Out of eighteen students, eight children speak English at home, five speak Spanish, two speak French, and three speak Tagalog.

Maddie's family speaks only English at home. Her parents want her to learn Spanish as a second language, so they enroll her in a Spanish-language immersion program where half the children are native Spanish speakers and the other half are native English speakers like Maddie.

Anya's family are refugees from Ukraine. She is the only child in her family child care whose first language is not English. Her parents hope to return home soon. They want her to learn English at school while remaining fluent in Ukrainian.

These scenarios are happening in early childhood programs across the United States and Canada, bringing challenges but also opportunities for directors and educators in programs large and small. Many multilingual learners are the children of new immigrant families learning English. Others come from English-speaking families who choose to send their children to a language immersion program where they will learn a second language. Consequently, children and staff with mixed language backgrounds interact in busy multilingual, multicultural classrooms. That can be exciting, but it also makes teaching complicated.

In the United States, we tend to categorize multilingual learners based on their reasons for learning multiple languages. Andy and Anya are considered circumstantial bilinguals. They are required to learn English so they can continue their education, as English is necessary for success in school and work in the United States. The purpose for learning English is pragmatic and functional. On the other hand, Maddie is seen as an elective bilingual. She is learning an additional language as a means of enriching her life experience socially and cognitively, without a sense of urgency. She is part of a growing group of children of affluent families who are pursuing the advantages of bilingualism (Williams 2017).

Yet the process of learning a new language (different from their home language) is the same for all children. I believe we should consider the situation for Andy and Anya to be a place of enrichment too, just like for Maddie—not just pragmatic and necessary. And we should recognize Maddie's position as a child who is asked to learn a new language outside of her familiar home environment—not just doing this for fun.

From the perspective of the children, the same educational and social-emotional best practices in teaching must be applied for all multilingual learners, regardless of their reasons for learning languages. The real goal is biliteracy, which is the ability to comprehend, speak, read, and write in both languages. For young children, oral language is the first crucial step, of course. So, in early childhood education, the emphasis must be on oral language as the foundation of early literacy. That means comprehension and speaking, but just as for monolingual speakers, the early literacy focus demands attention to early reading skills (phonological awareness, knowledge of the alphabet, and concepts of print) as well as early writing skills (Collins and Schickedanz 2024). With adequate scaffolding, all children will benefit from their multilingual education. It is a matter of equity.

In the pages that follow, I will offer sound ideas that are immediately usable with all young learners. Multilingual education is more complex than monolingual education. In the classroom, adults and children have to navigate using two or more languages throughout the day. While enriching, it also creates more opportunities for confusion. Why is an *apple* a *pomme* (French) or a *manzana* (Spanish)? And in which context do we use the correct word? This seems like a small issue, but it is not when we consider the many situations where language is used in an early childhood program by children as well as adults: reading books, telling stories, guiding children's behaviors, explaining rules, exchanging ideas, chatting about life, analyzing assessments, understanding safety regulations, eating together, and so on.

In workshops about teaching multilingual learners, I often ask participants to reflect on the joys and challenges they experience. This exercise always generates lively discussions. Educators talk about the joys:

> "It's wonderful to hear and see children who don't speak the same language learn to communicate in English as their common language now."

> "I enjoy having families come to my classroom to share their customs, songs, and stories."

> "I love sharing my culture from Colombia with the Anglo children and their families."

> "I feel like part of a bigger world."

Educators also share their challenges:

> "I am worried I cannot communicate with parents; they don't speak English, and I don't speak their language."

> "I am embarrassed I cannot speak English well, and the families don't understand what I say."

> "I have difficulty with discipline when the children don't follow my directions."

There is no doubt that being multilingual is a good thing. The cognitive benefits are real, as well as the social benefits (Baker and Wright 2021). But providing good multilingual education is more complicated than many proponents assume, whether it is English-speaking educators teaching children whose home language is not English, or educators whose home language is not English teaching English-speaking children.

If the objective is for the children to learn a language, it is not enough to immerse them in a linguistic bath with caring adults. The educators must be skilled at *teaching* the language:

- They must have knowledge of second language teaching and development.
- They must use specific teaching techniques to support the learning of a new language.
- They must have intentional strategies for honoring the home languages of the children.

The research points to the fact that the benefits of bilingualism are best realized when the children are taught well (Buysse et al. 2010; Goldenberg 2008; Wasik and Hindman 2011).

Bilingualism must be complemented with biliteracy, having not only social or conversational language but also academic language (Zelasko and Antunez 2000). For adults, conversational language is getting along in everyday life: shopping, chatting with friends, ordering in restaurants. Academic language is more formal and technical: reading voting rules on a ballot, discussing medical results with a doctor, filling out the paperwork to enroll a child in school.

For preschool children, social language is understanding the routines of the daily picture schedule, responding to the educator's direction to wash hands before lunch, and waving when their name is called at circle time. None of these activities requires elaborate use of words, as they depend mostly on the context. Academic language relies on a stronger knowledge and use of vocabulary. It is understanding the words in Eric Carle's *The Very Hungry Caterpillar*, such as *lollipop*, *Swiss cheese*, or *chocolate cake*, and using them in discussions of the story. It includes adding details in conversation, such as explaining how the caterpillar transforms into a butterfly. For getting ready to learn to read, academic language also means beginning to understand the rhyming sounds in *cat* and *bat*, as well as saying the letters in their name (Collins and Schickedanz 2024; Masterson 2022).

How the Book Is Organized

This book is for education leaders and classroom educators who are teaching multilingual learners. Whether you are new at it or you have been doing it for a while, I want to give you solid guidance on multilingual education. I hope you will find confirmation for what you are already doing well and also discover new ideas to try. Teaching all children requires intentionality. Teaching multilingual learners requires even more forethought because it involves more languages, more cultures, and therefore more complexity. I am confident the book will help answer your questions, ease your concerns, and give you a template for success.

The definitions section that follows this introduction and chapter 1 provide a common vocabulary for multilingual education and give the foundation to understand first and second language development.

Chapter 2 focuses on planning, an essential component of a good multilingual program.

Chapter 3 delves into working with families who are multilingual and multicultural.

Chapters 4 and 5 provide specific information on supporting educators, both monolingual and multilingual.

Chapter 6 addresses the importance of having an early literacy focus in the environment, curriculum, and materials.

Chapter 7 focuses on the explicit teaching of the second language.

Chapters 8 focuses on the explicit honoring of the children's home languages.

Chapter 9 describes ways to assess how the children are learning languages.

Chapter 10 addresses guiding the behavior of multilingual children.

The conclusion reflects on the creation of a multilingual, multicultural planet.

A checklist at the end of the book is your tool for planning programming for multilingual learners. You may want to start there. As you read each category and answer the statements on a scale of 1 to 3, you might identify areas of your program that need more immediate attention than others. Then you can go to the corresponding chapter and begin your planning.

Teaching Young Multilingual Learners focuses on the teaching and learning of a second language with a diversity and equity perspective for children, families, and educators (National Association for the Education of Young Children [NAEYC] 2019). It assumes that the reader is well informed about the overall concepts of developmentally appropriate principles and practices in early childhood education (NAEYC 2022). You can find additional information in the resources section at the end of this book.

I want this book to be simple and reassuring. My goal is to give you practical tips to gain confidence in these complex and common classroom situations.

> ## Definitions
>
> The language used to describe teaching multilingual education is changing. It seems important to start with some definitions so we share a common understanding in the space of this book. In recent years, the term has evolved from *English language learner* (ELL) to *dual language learner* (DLL) to the current *multilingual learner* (ML). You may discover new terms in your community that also apply. This is about not just thinking of children learning English as their second language but English-speaking children learning a target language such as Spanish or Mandarin in a language immersion school. The definitions below are organized by categories to help consolidate the concepts as much as possible.
>
> ### Multilingualism and Levels of Language Proficiency
>
> **Bilingualism:** knowing two languages.
>
> **Multilingualism:** knowing more than two languages.
>
> **Proficient bilingualism or multilingualism:** having the ability to comprehend, speak, read, and write in two or more languages.
>
> **Monolingual:** a person who knows one language.
>
> **Multilingual:** a person who knows more than one language. In the current lingo, it might be applied to a person speaking two languages (bilingual) or more than two languages.
>
> **Multilingual learner:** a person who is learning multiple languages. Realistically, learning several languages at the same time is rare, but *multilingual* is a preferred label in the field of education at the time of this writing.
>
> **Simultaneous learner:** a person learning two languages at the same time at home and/or at school.
>
> **Sequential learner:** a person learning a second language outside the home after having learned a first language.

Semilingualism: a term used to describe a situation in which individuals are not proficient in the languages they use; has been used politically to put down multilingualism. Such individuals may have a limited vocabulary, use incorrect grammar, or struggle to read or write fluently. This situation can occur for individuals who have a low educational level in their home language and who begin learning a second language by ear. To be proficient, most people need formal instruction.

Language Types

First language learning: the acquisition of a first language, usually organic in the context of family.

Second language learning: the acquisition of a second language; may happen in the family or in an outside program, and the family may or may not know the second language the child is learning.

Academic language: the language of learning, involving words not heard in daily conversations, such as in storybooks. It is the language of comparing, classifying, inferring, synthetizing, and analyzing. An example of academic language use by a four-year-old is describing the sequence of events in a story like "The Little Red Hen" or "Goldilocks and the Three Bears."

Social language: the language used in everyday life events, activities, and relationships. An example of social language for a four-year-old is talking about what happened during a visit to Grandma's house. Social language is sometimes called *conversational language*.

Expressive or productive language: language we speak to express what we think, want, feel, and need.

Receptive language: language we understand, even if we cannot necessarily speak it. Receptive language develops first in the process of learning a language, before expressive or productive language.

Pattern of second language learning: the general pattern of learning a second language that follows these steps or phases in sequential order: home language use, silent or listening period, telegraphic and formulaic speech, productive language use.

- **Home language use:** a phase of language learning when children continue to use their home language even in a second language environment.

- **Silent or listening period:** a phase of language learning when children keep quiet to observe and process what they hear.

- **Telegraphic or formulaic speech:** a phase of language learning when children show or point to objects or situations, use isolated words, or use two-word combinations.

- **Productive language use:** a phase of language learning when children know enough words and useful phrases to build their own sentences of three or more words.

Curriculum and Teaching Practices

Code switching: changing from one language (code) to another within one sentence or conversation, sometimes called *language mixing*. It happens often in informal conversation in families or with friends.

Language immersion: using one language of instruction exclusively, whether it is English or another language, for all the formal teaching, such as reading books, and the informal interactions, such as instructing children to put their coats on before recess.

Language introduction: a teaching practice that lets children know that there are other languages besides their home language and the language of instruction in their school. It develops metalinguistic awareness.

Language submersion: putting a child in a new language environment without warning or scaffolding, in a fail-or-succeed manner.

Metalinguistic awareness: the awareness that there is more than one word for each thought, action, or object; the ability to reflect on language and how it can be adapted and played with for different purposes. If I know French and English, I can tell you that a *dog* is the same as a *chien*, even though the words look and sound different.

Vocabulary: the words used by or known to individuals or groups of persons. We tend to have larger vocabulary in our areas of interest or in the languages we use most often. Vocabulary must be taught in the context of the topic of study or thematic unit. For example, there is a big body of words on the topic of "spring" that the children can learn, related to categories such as people, animals, location, qualifiers, foods, and objects. Rigorous teaching of a second language is about teaching vocabulary intentionally and coordinating the words to all centers of the classroom.

Additive vocabulary: combining vocabulary words that children know in their home language and in the new language they are learning. For example, they may say "the pájaro is blue" (the bird is blue). This shows that the child knows the concept (*pájaro* is a bird) but does not yet know the precise word for *bird* in English.

Thematic curriculum: a curriculum approach in which educators develop topics relevant to the children's lives, create a list of important words to learn for a given topic, provide materials, and propose activities with the objective of teaching vocabulary and encouraging children to practice their productive language.

Translanguaging: teaching technique that allows for the use of home language to complement the language of instruction without turning into random use of languages. For example, a teacher might use the technique of preview-view-review when reading a book. First they preview the story in a child's home language by giving a summary to prepare the child to understand the plot. Then they read the story in the target language. Finally, they discuss the story in the home language (and/or target language) to check for comprehension.

Linguistic goal: a goal that outlines the language or languages the program wants the children to learn. For example, the goal may be for the children to learn English or another target language.

Socio-cultural goal: a goal that outlines a positive approach for helping children learn about their own culture and the culture of others. For example, the goal may be for English-speaking children to learn about the culture of their classmates from other cultures and for newcomer children to learn about American culture.

CHAPTER 1: FIRST AND SECOND LANGUAGE DEVELOPMENT

Theo is eighteen months old. He is a monolingual English learner. Today he is in the playground with the toddler group. He sees a dog on the sidewalk behind the fence. He says, "Woof." His teacher responds, "Theo, you see a dog! It is a dog!" Theo looks up smiling and says, "Dog."

Esteban is four years old. He speaks Spanish at home and is learning English at preschool. As the teacher reads a book about horses, Esteban points to the picture and says, "Caballo." The teacher says, "Esteban, yes, you're right! Caballo is horse in English. Can you say horse?" Esteban concentrates and says, "Horse." The teacher acknowledges: "You know the word in Spanish—caballo—and in English—horse. Esteban, you are bilingual!" They high-five.

While Theo is learning in his home language and Esteban is learning a second language, the techniques their teachers use are similar. They respond to the children's attempts at communication. They expand on the children's knowledge. They give the children opportunities to practice. And they are enthusiastic about the children's language learning.

Considerations for Helping Children Acquire Language

There are two parts to language learning: the Language Acquisition Device (Chomsky 1965) and the Language Acquisition Support System (Bruner 1983).

The Language Acquisition Device (LAD) is the instinctive mental capacity that young humans have to acquire and produce language from birth. Some people say that babies are wired for language, as if babies know that their survival depends on their ability to communicate. And in fact, it does, and it starts with crying as the first sign of distress an infant can make. When a baby cries, an adult comes to the rescue. The LAD has a predictable pattern. First children are in a prelinguistic stage then they move to babbling. Infants are very good at imitating the rhythm and the intonation of the language they're hearing. Then follows the first-word stage, the two-words stage, the telegraphic stage, and then productive language. By the time they are six years old, typically developing children can make six- to eight-word sentences easily: "Today I go to my grandma's house."

The Language Acquisition Support System (LASS) is the support from adults that children get as they progress in the development of language. It is the social interactions that stimulate the children to listen, respond, and talk. It is jointly reading picture books with adults. It is the positive reinforcement babies get when they first utter the sound *da* and their father smiles and says, "Yes, da, da, daddy. I am your daddy!" It is when a child learning English points to a picture and says "ball" and the teacher excitedly says "Yes, you're right, in English it is a ball!" And it is the attention that children get for their sentences: "Oh, you are going to your grandma's house! That will be fun! What will you do there?"

In learning a second language, there is also a predictable sequence: use of the first language, silent or listening period, formulaic speech, and productive language use (Tabors 2008). When children first arrive in a classroom where the instruction is happening in a different language than their first language, they tend to continue to speak their home language. It has worked for them in the past, so they have no reason to believe it will not work for them in a new situation. But they soon find out that what they say is not understood or even is ignored. This usually leads to a silent period in which the children go about their business nonverbally. They may point or use gestures but do not say words. This is a valuable time of learning, as children observe and listen, figuring out what is going on around them. They are building receptive vocabulary as they understand more and more words but are not yet able to say them.

Once they have enough vocabulary, with gentle encouragement from adults and other children, they begin to use formulas and actions that they have seen used successfully by others. They might use telegraphic speech: one-word sentences like "Truck" accompanied by pointing to a truck, or interjections like "Hey!" to get someone's attention. The one-word stage generally grows into sentences with two or three words: "Me want milk." This happens best when children have a strong LASS that stimulates them to talk in their second language, just like it does for their first language.

Sometimes educators wonder what to do during the silent stage and choose to leave the children alone until they are ready to talk on their own. Providing low-key but frequent opportunities for practice using the target language is a more supportive strategy, especially for quiet children who might not volunteer to talk. If children do not have enough practice talking (expressive language), they can gain a level of receptive language that allows them to figure things out, but they do not progress well enough to achieve proficiency in expressive language.

We *could* assert that it is easy to be a bilingual baby. The level of language needed for infants to communicate is mostly receptive. It is also easy to be a bilingual toddler who points and says one word. The language output and input at these ages is still simple. But it becomes challenging for preschoolers who have an increasing need to say what they think, want, know, and feel. Without the ability to manipulate the right words for a situation, they are at risk of staying at the toddler stage of language development in the second language.

Second language learning is natural, but it is a challenging task. According to research, with proper support it takes five to seven years of sustained study to acquire academic language in a second language (Castro et al. 2013; Cummins 1979; Genesee 2016). It is very similar to learning to play a musical instrument, isn't it? Yet the majority of teachers expect young children to reach native-like English proficiency effortlessly and largely without instruction (Genesee 2016). The popular message and the optimistic descriptions of immersion programs reinforce the myth of children learning language "like sponges." The danger is that educators who hold this belief are less likely to support multilingual learners through the language learning process. They assume that just immersing the children in a language is enough for them to speak it.

When visiting multilingual preschool classrooms, observers often note that they are quieter than monolingual classrooms. The children are busy, playing with toys, but they do not talk with one another much. There is no arguing in the dramatic play area or negotiating in the block area or comparing shapes at the playdough table. The difference is that the children do not have enough common language to talk with one another about what they think, want, know, and feel. If the goal is for children to be multilingual, educators must increase the opportunities for children to use their expressive language. They do so by engaging the children in discussions and conversations, as described in chapters 6, 7, and 8.

Multilingual learners need planned and systematic support that focuses on language for academic and social purposes as well as honoring their home language (Genesee 2016). They need a strong LASS for the target language, using the intentional pedagogy of translanguaging without code switching or mixing languages randomly.

Code switching vs. translanguaging

Let's look at the difference between code switching and translanguaging. Code switching is going from one language to another in a way that an outside listener would find random. For example, a teacher might say: "*Toma las* balls. *Vamos a jugar en el* playground" (Take the balls. We are going to play in the playground). Some words are in English and others in Spanish, in a seamless sentence of Spanglish. This approach is heard often within families or social conversations, and that is OK. It is a legitimate way to communicate at home and with friends informally. However, if used in all aspects of life, it becomes semilingualism, where the speaker is not able to carry on a conversation in any one language correctly.

Educators should not code switch languages randomly in the classroom. The classroom is a formal environment where teaching and learning take place. We want children and adults to become proficient in speaking, reading, and writing in English, as well as any other languages being taught. That equips children to move on to the academic world of school and work. Thus, languages must be differentiated.

Avoiding code switching, educators can use a pedagogy called *translanguaging*. This intentional teaching strategy allows the child to use their home language to comprehend or expand their second language. We see that in the example of Esteban in the vignette at the beginning of the chapter. As he uses Spanish (what he knows) to talk about the horse, the teacher respects that previous knowledge. Then she teaches him the word in English. By acknowledging the act of learning the second language, the teacher gives Esteban the confidence to continue the effort.

Applying a Diversity and Equity Lens

The NAEYC position statement on Advancing Equity in Early Childhood Education (2019) recommends that we focus on children's strengths. This means paying attention to children's previous knowledge and assessing their current knowledge so educators can augment or scaffold new learning. We must recognize what children already know in their first language. We must respect that they are not sponges, passively absorbing a language, but rather active learners working hard to acquire the new language, with their brains on high alert as they make sense of what is said to them and around them—assessing the context, understanding what they have heard, and then responding by choosing actions, saying words, and making sentences that let them be understood. Focusing on strength means trusting in the children's drive and resilience to learn a second language with us, even as their first language is still in development. We must offer them many opportunities to practice: through rigorous teaching, in playful ways, and in the social environment of the classroom.

Practical Strategies for Promoting First and Second Language Development

1. Keep the concepts of the LASS at the forefront to develop both children's first and second languages with confidence. That means always being ready and intentional to support children's attempts at communicating, however small they are.

2. Respond when children initiate communication, whether it is verbal or nonverbal. If a child points silently to a bird on a tree, say: "You see a bird! I see the bird too!" If a child says a one-word sentence such as "Bird," say, "Yes, you see the bird! It is a blue bird!"

3. Show enthusiasm for language and words in books. As you read *The Very Hungry Caterpillar*, for example, point to word length ("Listen to this word: *cat-er-pil-lar*. It is a long word. Let's say it together again! Now let's listen to a short word in this book, *leaf*. Let's say it together! Leaf!").

4. Invite children into conversations by commenting on their actions: "You are climbing on the slide"; "Your tower is tall. It has five blocks!" Giving words is a practical way to increase vocabulary.

5. Invite children into conversations by commenting on their emotions: "You are sad because mommy left. She will be back soon!" "You are proud that you finished the puzzle."

6. Wait five to eight seconds after speaking to children to give them time to think and reply with their own words.

7. Give positive feedback so children know they are communicating successfully. "You can say *manzana* in Spanish and *apple* in English. You are bilingual!"

8. Model communication in one language at a time and avoid switching languages randomly. Rather than saying, "It's time to wash *las manos*," say, "It's time to wash our hands."

9. Use translanguaging as intentional pedagogy that respects the child's previous knowledge. For example, as you read a book about bears, and a child points and says, "*Oso*" (*bear* in Spanish), you would respond, "Yes, you are right. It is an oso! It is a bear! *Oso* in Spanish, *bear* in English! Can you say *bear*?" As the child repeats, you would say, "A *bear*, *un oso*—you speak Spanish and English. Fantastic!"

10. Talk about being multilingual to build pride in the children's accomplishment of knowing more than one language: "In this classroom we speak several languages. We all speak English. And Maria and Toni speak Spanish too, and Ivana speaks Ukrainian. We are multilingual!"

CHAPTER 2: PLANNING PROGRAMS

With little advance notice, six immigrant children have enrolled in director Karina's program. At home they speak Spanish, Arabic, and French. Their parents have limited English proficiency. Director Karina considers how to support her teachers and make the classrooms welcoming for children and families. At first she worries that she does not have the resources to accomplish this. Then she makes a plan with several steps: addressing teachers' concerns, identifying the goals for the children, inventorying the materials, providing training and coaching, engaging families, and reviewing the curriculum to adapt it to better include the children into the overall program. Not everything can be done at once, so she starts with addressing teachers' concerns so they can inform her overall plan. In this case, the teachers wanted help with increasing children's comprehension of English for transitions during the day. Karina found a website with practical suggestions that was immediately useful: the Multilingual Learning Toolkit, www.multilinguallearningtoolkit.org.

Los Niños Spanish Immersion child care center has opened to great success. English-speaking families in the area want their children to grow up multilingual. Most of the staff come from various countries in Latin America and speak Spanish as their first language. Most families do not speak Spanish. At drop-off and pickup time, parents and educators exchange information quickly with simple greeting words, but when families have a question, they go to the English-speaking director. Interpreters are present for family-teacher conferences, but some educators feel embarrassed by this situation. The director begins offering Friday evening English language lessons. Staff enthusiasm is high, and soon it is evident more English language support is needed. Going further, the director organizes English as a second language (ESL) classes through the local public school agency, which offers free in-person and online classes. The goal of the program is to improve the staff's English language skills so they are better able to communicate with families and increase their professional confidence.

Considerations for Planning a Program for Multilingual Learners

Educators worry about children not understanding directions or not fitting in because they cannot communicate. They also wonder about how to support home languages they do not speak. They need reassurance that their leaders will support them in this task by problem solving and finding resources. Families are eager for their children to do well. They hope for the best education for their children, and by enrolling them in your program, they expect the best services.

As we see with director Karina, a planning mindset is essential because it helps you find answers. If you are a director or leader, you already have a lot of experience planning for the children in the program. Planning for the special needs of multilingual learners does require extra time and resources. The checklist on pages 49–53 at the end of this book is a planning tool to help you assess the areas in which to focus for your program.

It is more complicated to have a multilingual classroom or program than a monolingual English one. Multiple languages must be supported in different ways: procuring materials and adapting teaching strategies; hiring and coaching multilingual staff; providing professional development to all staff, monolingual and multilingual; and facilitating engagement of families who may or may not speak the target language. Consequently, the cost is higher. The director should not ignore the added expenses of multilingual teaching and must be intentional in the budgeting.

While a monolingual program requires a professional development plan for common topics like child development, safety, and curriculum, a multilingual program must add the language component for children as well as for staff. Educators who are monolingual English speakers need training to work with families who do not speak English. Educators who speak other languages but are not proficient in English need help working with English-speaking families, as illustrated in the vignette about Los Niños Spanish Immersion program. These educators often feel undervalued as low-status workers who care for children of affluent families. They need support to improve their English proficiency so they can build their professional status.

Applying a Diversity and Equity Lens

The NAEYC position statement on Advancing Equity in Early Childhood Education (2019) recommends paying attention to the special characteristics of providing high-quality programs for diverse populations such as multilingual learners. The goals of equity require commitment and concrete actions that include being proactive in planning, tailoring instruction, recruiting and training educators, fostering a learning community, and engaging families. This means realizing that multilingual programs will look different from monolingual ones in areas of staffing, curriculum, and family support. It also means rearranging budgets to meet the needs of children, families, and staff.

Practical Strategies for Planning Programs for Multilingual Learners

1. Take the time to plan for teaching multilingual learners even if you have a small program. You have to determine the resources you have in order to know what you need. The amount of preparation will depend on the number of children you are serving and the languages children speak at home. For example, it is easier in the United States to find resources in Spanish than in other languages.

2. Budget the cost of teaching multilingual learners. This strategy is high on the list because it is foundational for every other aspect. It is more expensive to run a multilingual program than a monolingual program. There are several extras to consider, such as time for planning, materials such as books in home languages, tailored professional development, and interpreters and translators. While this may seem scary, this reality is manageable with intentional planning. Some steps can alleviate the cost, such as asking cultural associations to donate books in home languages or seeking grants for professional development workshops.

3. Listen to staff concerns and engage staff in planning. This can be done in group meetings or individually, depending on the circumstances. The goal is for everyone to feel confident that they will receive the support they need, whether it is training, books, or help with adapting the curriculum.

4. Invest in professional development of educators to increase their skills and their sense of competence. They may need more information on a particular topic like behavior guidance or early literacy for teaching the children. Or they may need to enroll in an adult ESL class to improve their professional ability to communicate with families.

5. Get to know the children and families. Learn about the languages they speak at home. Find out their reasons for enrolling their children in your program. It may be practical, such as being the closest center to their home. Or it may be philosophical, such as their desire for their children to learn a second language.

6. Set linguistic goals for the children. With the help of families, decide what you want the children to learn. Will it be an introduction to the language, or will the children be proficient at an age-appropriate level? Identifying linguistic goals will help you plan the curriculum.

7. Set socio-cultural goals for the children. With the help of families, decide how you want the children to perceive themselves and others as members of a caring multilingual community. Do you want the children to develop a positive identity within the English cultural group, their home language cultural groups, or both? Thinking about this will help you develop the children's intercultural awareness.

8. Adapt the curriculum to meet the linguistic and socio-cultural goals you have for children. For example, multilingual children will need longer exposure to a topic or unit of study to learn vocabulary, so it will be necessary to increase the length from the standard expectation to have more time to practice listening and speaking the language.

9. Provide extra paid time for adapting the curriculum and instruction, for example, for finding books in home languages or preparing for family conferences in collaboration with an interpreter.

10. Enrich your curriculum by scheduling staff, family, and community speakers to come to your program to share their languages. For example, you may not have a classroom staff member who speaks Vietnamese, but you can connect with a local Vietnamese American organization to have a volunteer read to the children.

CHAPTER 3: WORKING WITH FAMILIES

In this bilingual Spanish–English preschool, there are two distinct populations: a high-income, highly educated group of English-speaking families and a low-income group of Spanish-speaking immigrants with little formal education. The program's governing board is committed to providing equitable education and access for all. Through active fundraising, generous scholarships are provided to some children while others pay full tuition. The instruction is bilingual, with Spanish in the morning and English in the afternoon. This week, director Ana has two family conferences with different situations to address. An English-speaking family wants to know how much Spanish their children will be able to speak on a trip to Costa Rica. An immigrant family wants to know whether their child will be ready for kindergarten at the local public school. Each family has expectations based on their hopes for their child and in response to the claims of the school that the children will be bilingual. In preparing for the conferences, Ana tailors her comments to each family's interest. Her explanations include examples of the educational approach the program is using to work toward each child's goals.

Considerations for Working with Families of Multilingual Learners

Families' expectations for their children come with little formal knowledge of the language acquisition process. They hope that their child will learn the second language simply and effortlessly, as naturally as they learn their home language. They often have unrealistic ideas about their child's abilities and progress. Educators should have knowledge of first language and second language development so they can explain to families the sequence for learning a second language and the techniques they use for teaching. Educators can also give families tips to maintain the home language at home and suggestions for reinforcing the second language if the families do not speak it themselves.

According to research, children need to have about 30 percent of their daily interactions in a second language to learn it, adding up to about twenty-five hours a week (Pearson 2008). This is not just listening but also producing or speaking that language. Based on this general formula, we can extrapolate that children almost certainly will not get enough time to practice speaking the new language in the classroom to become proficient. They are likely to develop receptive language but not enough expressive language to be fluent. Therefore, it is important to give families ideas and tips to reinforce the language at home and in the community outside of the program.

Early education practices vary across the world. Educators play a key role in helping immigrant and newcomer families understand how their program operates. The arrangement of your classroom, with an abundance of toys and materials, colors, and activities, may be a new experience for newcomer families. They may be disconcerted by practices such as health regulations, expectations for family involvement, and your daily schedule. Soon they will get used to it and like it, but they need to be welcomed with gentle guidance so they feel comfortable in the program.

Applying a Diversity and Equity Lens

The NAEYC position statement on Advancing Equity in Early Childhood Education (2019) recommends establishing reciprocal relationships with families by working with the family to learn more about them, identifying common goals, and establishing strategies to meet those goals. The universal goal for all families is that children will be ready for kindergarten. In multilingual programs, there is the added goal of language learning. This goal is sometimes ignored under the assumption that children magically pick up language. So it's important to be attentive to each family's circumstances, as described in the vignette at the beginning of this chapter. For some families, the language goal is to learn English well. For others, it is to learn the second language well. Educators must demonstrate to families how they teach language, specifically the techniques they use and the progress the children are making.

This article from NAEYC helps explain some common jargon used in early childhood education: www.naeyc.org/our-work/families/12-teacher-terms-demystified.

Practical Strategies for Working with Families

1. Use plain English to communicate with families verbally and in writing. This helps families understand the jargon of early childhood education and makes it easier for translators and interpreters.

2. Host informational events for families to explain how children learn first and second languages. Explain how the process of language learning has phases. As explained in chapter 2, learning a second language starts with children continuing to speak their home language. Then they go into the silent phase, during which they do not talk but try to figure out what is happening. Then they move to a telegraphic and formulaic phase, with words like "OK," or "Stop, stop." When children have more knowledge and confidence, they begin productive language, first with simple one- or two-word sentences like "Me milk," and then becoming more complex: "I am thirsty. I want to drink milk."

3. Explain to families how you teach the target language. Let parents know the techniques you use to teach vocabulary, such as pointing to pictures in the book, explaining the words, and having the children repeat the words, then continuing the learning later through repeated use of these words in play or in songs (explained in chapter 7).

4. Reassure families that their child is learning English or the target second language by showing them examples of children's work. It might include a dictation on a drawing, a short audio of the child talking or singing, or a video of children in dramatic play using the target language.

5. Use technology to link their home language stories with the classroom curriculum themes. For example, if you are studying the topic of transportation, use the classroom communication app to ask families to send a picture or video related to transportation that you can then share with all children in the classroom. It may be about their car or about how they ride a city bus to go shopping on weekends.

6. Organize families to participate in the classroom, for example, sharing a song, a dish, or a book in their home language.

7. Invite families for educational and social events, such as a book reading afternoon, game night, or Saturday morning sing-along in the target language. This is a positive way to foster the sense of being a multilingual, multicultural community.

8. Give immigrant/non-English-speaking families tips for maintaining their home language in the dominant English environment. With your help, families can design a language plan. Depending on the skills of parents or other family members, they

might choose to speak the home language at home and English outside the home or have one adult speak the home language and another adult English.

9. Give families of English-speaking children in your immersion program a realistic picture of what their child is learning. Share tips to increase exposure in the target language at home, such as watching videos, reading board books, attending community events, or using a language learning app such as Duolingo together.

10. Provide families with materials in the target language for home use. You could offer a lending library of books, coloring pages, toys, and games. Encourage families to donate items for the lending library, which also builds their sense of belonging to the multilingual community.

CHAPTER 4: SUPPORTING MONOLINGUAL EDUCATORS

Teacher Alex has three children who are learning English in her classroom. At home they speak Tamil, Spanish, and Japanese. Their parents want the children to learn English while they continue speaking their home language at home. Alex wonders if that will be confusing for the children.

When the children first enter the center, Alex notices that the children seem scared or confused. After a few days, they start acting up during transitions, crying and refusing to cooperate. She worries about communication. Her director tells her to use the Google Translate app to tell the children what to do, and all will work out. But it does not work well. It is confusing for the children to hear their teacher talking while holding a cell phone with a different voice.

Next, the director brings in a consultant who gives helpful advice: go slow and speak slowly, be friendly (smile and use a warm tone), be direct in transitions (give children time to understand, lead them by the hand), and explain the classroom routines to parents (so they can talk with their children). Following these tips helps Alex relax. The children relax too. After a few weeks, everyone is reassured, and routines are smoother. Soon Alex receives additional training to learn specific instructional techniques for teaching English.

Considerations for Supporting Monolingual Educators

Educators usually see learning more than one language in a positive light. They believe the research that multilingualism is good for children academically and socially. They are welcoming of the children coming in their classroom. At the same time, like teacher Alex in the opening vignette, they have legitimate concerns that should be addressed.

Some of these concerns are practical, such as questions surrounding behavior guidance and curriculum:

> "How will the children be able to follow the routines of the classroom?"
>
> "How will the children understand the book at story time if they don't know English?"
>
> "Do I have enough materials in the home language to honor the children's language?"
>
> "Will there be speakers of the home languages to help in teaching the children and communicating with families?"

Educators also want to know more about language acquisition. Monolingual people tend to be unaware of language (Bialystok 2001). They do not have reason to reflect or compare languages, so they don't think much about it. They may have had second language instruction in school when they were students themselves, but now they have forgotten that language without consequences. As teachers, then, they do not have full understanding of what it takes to learn and continue to practice a second language. Yet it takes more than merely speaking to children in the target language for children to learn. It takes explicit instruction with explicit strategies (Zelasko and Antunez 2000). Monolingual educators thus benefit greatly from tailored professional development on teaching a second language.

Some educators may have conflicting opinions about immigration. They may feel resentful of immigrants, or, on the other hand, they may feel guilty that they are not doing enough to help immigrants. The program leaders must acknowledge these feelings and concerns of educators so they can move confidently into teaching multilingual learners.

Programs must provide in-service training to increase educators' skills and support their confidence in teaching multilingual children and in working with multilingual colleagues in the classroom. This training must go beyond philosophy and give practical tips on *how* to teach. The theory is important, but practical tips are more useful and a great relief for monolingual educators.

Programs also must provide training for working in multilingual teams. In many early childhood programs, monolingual educators work side by side with educators or community members who speak another language, and who may speak English with varying degrees of proficiency. Although little information is available on this topic for the field of early childhood education, multilingualism is a growing phenomenon in corporate settings where workers of different languages collaborate in person or virtually. Multilingual teams need to pay special attention to communication. They have to work harder at communication than monolingual teams who are skilled in the same language. Fluent English speakers may have limited patience with colleagues who are less proficient. Misunderstandings, conflicts, and feelings of isolation can flare up and affect team performance.

Applying a Diversity and Equity Lens

The NAEYC position statement on Advancing Equity in Early Childhood Education (2019) recommends providing regular time and space to foster a positive learning community. That applies to a monolingual team, and perhaps even more so to a multilingual team, which includes monolingual and multicultural educators working together. While we tend to think of equity for children, we must expand our thinking to include monolingual educators. It is not fair to assume that without adequate information and support they know how to teach multilingual learners well or how to work with colleagues from other cultures. They benefit from professional development to explore cultural beliefs and responsiveness as well as techniques to enhance teaching skills. They need time and space for reflection. Children's well-being and learning is dependent on all educators' skills and professional competence.

Practical Strategies for Supporting Monolingual Educators

1. Listen to educators' concerns. Educators may have worries about communicating with the children and their families because they want to do a good job. Pay attention to the questions they pose or the situations they describe. Are they worried about behavior, materials and resources, or working with families?

2. Provide professional development on second language learning. The myth that second language learning is effortless for children is hard to let go. It is essential for monolingual speakers to understand the process and recognize the efforts children are making.

3. Provide professional development on practical teaching strategies, such as reading books, singing, giving directions, greeting children, following routines, and working with small and large groups. Chapters 6, 7, and 8 provide details on these strategies.

4. Provide professional development on cultural awareness in a multilingual, multicultural setting to alleviate the potential for miscommunication. Focus on team building, using plain English, best practices for use of translation tools, and fostering a culture of patience and empathy.

5. Encourage monolingual educators to take a short course in the languages the children speak. Your community may have free or low-cost options. Although it is not always feasible, and the goal definitely is not becoming fluent, this opportunity can be well received by educators who begin to have a better sense of what it is like to learn other languages. You can also engage in simple practices on-site to increase engagement with other languages, such as spending a staff meeting watching a video of a children's book being read in a language other than English.

6. Schedule follow-ups to the professional development training with a system for continuing to exchange ideas and strategies. One idea is to hang a poster in the teacher's lounge with the title "Strategies that work in my classroom with multilingual learners . . ." or "I still have these questions about teaching multilingual learners . . ."

7. Coach educators to adapt their lesson plans to the needs of multilingual learners. Look to chapters 6, 7, 8, 9, and 10 for suggestions based on their situations. Coaching may be done individually or as classroom teaching teams.

8. Have a solid evaluation and support plan for educators that includes time for observation, feedback, and coaching, in addition to information on best practices. For more information, see *Evaluating and Supporting Early Childhood Teachers* by Angèle Sancho Passe (2015).

9. Acknowledge that it is an extra challenge to teach multilingual learners, whether there is one isolated child learning English or whether the classroom is "superdiverse" with multiple languages in addition to English as the common language. Reward the challenge by providing extra paid time for lesson planning and adapting materials.

10. Budget for the extra time and resources necessary for lesson planning, coordinating with multilingual colleagues, and additional professional development, individual coaching, and team building. Funding may come from the existing budget or community, public, or private resources.

CHAPTER 5: SUPPORTING MULTILINGUAL EDUCATORS

Fasiya is a cultural navigator in a school readiness program. Her job is to support multilingual learners and their families. She is a caring worker who knows her community well. She has native oral proficiency in her home language, although her writing skills are limited. Her ability to speak and write in English is low. She feels competent when working with families in their home language. She is nervous in staff meetings as she does not understand all that is being said and she cannot contribute easily.

Maria is a lead teacher in a Spanish immersion program. She has a teaching degree from her native Peru. She has proficient reading skills in English, but her speech is not fluent. While she feels confident teaching the children, she dreads communicating with families, as she is intimidated by parents who ask questions about child development. For family-teacher conferences, the director hires an interpreter. That adds to Maria's embarrassment.

Both Fasiya and Maria are serious individuals with a desire to grow professionally. With that in mind, their directors put plans in place to increase their professional skills and their knowledge of early childhood education. They attend professional development sessions with their colleagues, and they get additional coaching by a program mentor to process the information. As part of their professional advancement plan, they also attend free ESL classes for adults in the school district. As they continue to improve in their English literacy and early education skills, they report increased job satisfaction and pride in their accomplishments.

Considerations for Supporting Multilingual Educators

The ideas in the previous chapter for supporting monolingual educators apply to this chapter too. Here I want to add a few ideas that are more tailored to multilingual educators. First, let's examine who these multilingual workers are. Some are individuals born in the United States (or Canada) who are fluent in English and another language and who have established credentials for teaching, such as a Child Development Associate (CDA) certification or state teaching license.

Other multilingual educators are new immigrants who have formal training in education from their home country, with teaching experience ranging from early education to higher education. Now in your program, they must learn on the job the idiosyncratic characteristics of early childhood education in your country and your specific context, such as health and safety regulations; family engagement strategies; curriculum expectations; privacy rules; diversity, equity, inclusion, and belonging philosophy; and so on.

The child care field is frequently an entry point to the workforce for new immigrants. Accordingly, many multilingual educators come to the early childhood workforce with little or no previous experience. They bring cultural and personal sensitivity to children and families from their same background. However, they may not have the teaching skills or the English language skills needed to do the job well. For example, they may not be able to read to children even in their home language if they have low literacy skills.

According to a report on the Demographic Characteristics of the Early Care and Education Workforce (Paschall et al. 2020), the number of multilingual early educators differs by community in the United States. In high-density immigrant areas, about 26 percent of workers in child care centers are born outside the country, and 47 percent of family child care providers. In low-density immigrant areas, the numbers are 5 percent for child care centers and 25 percent for family child care. Based on the immediate geographical area, each program has individual variables to consider in planning professional development for multilingual educators.

The professional development needs of multilingual educators vary. Essentially, some may not be multilingual yet, still more or less monolingual in their home language. Therefore, the support must be tailored to their specific individual needs, be it improving their teaching skills, their English oral language skills, their literacy skills, or a combination. For example, if an educator's pronunciation makes it difficult to understand what they are saying, early childhood programs must offer training to improve these skills. Speaking is oral language, and an accent is not a personal trait. Accent is a skill that can be learned, and there are many resources in the community to help, such as ESL classes for adult learners.

Often multilingual workers are hired for their language skills, without a clear job description. Program leaders must have a plan for their employment so they feel valuable in the classroom. They will be most effective when they understand clearly when to use their home language for instruction. Not only is it essential for the professional growth and confidence of the multilingual educators, but it is also necessary for the overall quality of education in the program. Children need educators who are role models for literate multilingualism and who can speak and read proficiently in their home language and in English.

Applying a Diversity and Equity Lens

The NAEYC position statement on Advancing Equity in Early Childhood Education (2019) recommends employing staff who speak the language of the children while also meeting professional expectations. Programs that hire multilingual educators become multilingual, multicultural workplaces. Equity means that everyone is welcomed and will be guided into fitting in professionally and personally. The same attention that is paid to children and families must be paid to workers, who deserve a caring workplace community and a system to enhance their professional competence. They must receive recognition for the positives they bring to the program. They also should receive appropriate guidance such as regular evaluation and support so they can do a good job and so they can improve their skills. This tailored approach may require extra resources, but it provides many benefits to their programs and the children these educators care for.

Practical Strategies for Supporting Multilingual Educators

1. Hire with care. The person may have nice qualities and speak the appropriate language for the context but lack other necessary skills for educating children. Be clear on the expectations for the job and immediately begin a professional development plan to get each worker's skills updated.

2. Have a job description for multilingual workers that specifies their role. This may depend on the worker's skills and experience as well as on the number of children in the program who speak the same language.

3. Create a language plan for when the home language will be used. Multilingual educators will use home languages for specific instructional purposes, such as honoring children in greetings, songs, or reading books, or in using the translanguaging technique described in chapter 1. Also, they can use the home language for comfort when a child is upset.

4. Integrate multilingual workers into a caring community of workers where all are valued, centering around the issue of language specifically. That means consciously being tolerant and respectful of accents and cultural backgrounds.

5. Be aware of feelings of isolation and exclusion for non-native speakers who may be hesitant to speak English one-on-one or in meetings. Facilitate their participation by giving them a voice and space to add their ideas.

6. Encourage and model plain language. Jargon, idioms, and slang can easily lead to confusion. Be conscious of speaking clearly and slowly and giving multilingual staff extra time for responding.

7. Do not allow gossip. The field of early education is a people business, which can lead to being lax about confidentiality and boundaries. Multilingual teams are especially vulnerable when members of the same language group talk to one another without others understanding what they are saying. Explain that gossip does not just hurt staff but harms the education of children as they feel the tension among adults.

8. Be explicit about using English as the common professional language for all staff. At the same time, it may be necessary to make accommodations by offering training in home languages, or, as for children, using translanguaging to increase comprehension. For example, give the presentation in English for all staff, and then hold small-group discussions of the topic in home languages.

9. Promote collaboration and team building among all educators, monolingual and multilingual, with informal activities such as sharing songs or treats at staff meetings. Hold formal training workshops that focus on language and culture.

10. Hold the multilingual educators to the same professional standards and practices as monolingual educators while scaffolding their linguistic skills.

CHAPTER 6: THE ENVIRONMENT, CURRICULUM, AND MATERIALS

Min and Pierre are in the block corner. They are making tunnels and bridges for the small cars and trucks to navigate. Min speaks Korean at home, and Pierre speaks Haitian Creole. At school they are learning the vocabulary of transportation with this month's curriculum. It is an exciting time as they are both very much interested in the topic. Their teacher's goal is to get them to go past "wroom-wroom" interactions. He makes it a point to teach key words during story time, using the vocabulary from books such as Good Night Cars by Adam Gamble and Mark Jasper and Maisy Goes on a Plane by Lucy Cousins. They learn big words like taxi cab, roadway, lift off, and departure gate. As their teacher walks by them during active learning, he hears Min say, "Pierre, look! Taxi cab go to airport." Min responds, "Airplane go up, lift off." Both Min and Pierre laugh. While the conversation appears disjointed, it shows that the boys' vocabulary is increasingly sophisticated. They are learning English! Their teacher has coordinated the learning for them: the environment, the curriculum, and the materials are integrated into a coherent whole so they can practice talking as they play.

Considerations for the Environment, Curriculum, and Materials for Multilingual Learners

As shown in the vignette, the focus in a multilingual program has to be early literacy in all the aspects of the classroom: environment, curriculum, and materials. Children spend a long time in their early childhood program. To learn, they must feel safe and calm and have a sense of belonging. That means finding familiar sights and sounds that they can recognize. They also are in the program to discover new ideas, people, toys, and experiences. They need an environment that provides "mirrors" and "windows" (Sims Bishop 1990).

"Mirrors" are ways for children to see and hear themselves. Hearing their home languages in songs and reading is a "mirror" too. It reinforces what they know and who they are.

"Windows" are about learning new things, primarily language for second language learners but also for learning new concepts like science and math. They expand children's experience of the world beyond what they already know from their family life.

Educators must be intentional in setting the environment and the curriculum so it is a bridge between home and school. That is accomplished by involving families and children so that they bring their ideas to the curriculum.

The more home and school activities are similar, the easier it is for children to follow along and participate. While children can eventually figure things out on their own, teachers can facilitate the learning faster by teaching explicitly what they want children to know. As in the vignette, the teacher teaches vocabulary that is specific to the play so the children have words to use. Once they know some of the words, they will expand on their own. But they need the seeds to begin.

Center time, free play, or active learning is normally when children explore independently. They are engaged in hands-on activities. As they play with their peers, they develop social skills such as sharing and negotiating. In a multilingual classroom, children are hindered by their lack of common language so they often play silently. Multilingual learners need the facilitation of adults to give them the words to increase their vocabulary and enrich their play.

The same is true for informal parts of the day like mealtimes and outdoor play. It is not enough for children to follow routines and exercise their bodies. Educators must consider language throughout the day, such as saying, "Leo, you are running fast," or "Hamed, look, the carrots are orange and the broccoli is green." These tiny teachable moments are the building blocks of language learning.

Applying a Diversity and Equity Lens

The NAEYC position statement on Advancing Equity in Early Childhood Education (2019) recommends actively involving children and families in the design and implementation of learning activities. While educators show the children what is expected of them in the classroom, in turn they must also realize that what children already know from home can be adapted to the classroom. Rather than relying on commercial, stereotypical ethnic toys and materials, educators should involve children and families in cocreating the environment, as well as selecting the materials. For example, rather than educators alone building a bakery for the dramatic play center, they can invite families and children to share ideas and artifacts, involving them in deciding which baked goods will be sold. Then, based on the makeup of the group, the project may turn out to be a classic *panadería* or a truly international *bakery* (English)/*panadería* (Spanish)/*boulanjri* (Haitian Creole). Imagine how many new words the children are learning and the conversations they can have! Not only is it an excellent exercise in early literacy that enriches the learning of vocabulary and concepts, but it is also a way to affirm the children's cultural backgrounds.

Practical Strategies to Focus on Early Literacy in the Environment, Curriculum, and Materials

1. Offer mirrors by using children's home language for greetings and some activities. Have books that illustrate their families' stories as well as toys that are familiar to them. Post children's drawings and dictations at eye level. Provide actual mirrors so they can see themselves and their classmates literally.

2. Offer windows. The first obvious "window" is the new language they are learning. You are giving them a positive window by using the language in an explicitly friendly way, showing the patience to allow them to practice, followed by your joyful responses as they learn to understand and express themselves in this new tongue.

3. Integrate the curriculum with themes and projects to ground the vocabulary, or the set of words that apply to a given topic. Think about vocabulary as a web with categories of words for people, foods, animals, descriptors, places, objects, actions, and feelings. For example, if the topic is bears, you will have words for people (ranger, zookeeper), foods (berries, fish), animals (cub, polar bear), descriptors (brown, furry), places (forest, den), objects (log, bee, hive), actions (eat, hibernate), and feelings (fear, love). Develop your vocabulary list from the books you are reading at circle time. Then use these words at other times of the day. At lunch you might say, "We are eating blueberries for dessert today. Bears like blueberries too!"

4. Use repetition as a critical tool for learning. At story time, use a repeated-read-aloud technique and read the same book several days a week. Rather than being bored, children get excited about understanding more of the story as the days progress. By the fourth reading, many will have learned enough words to chime in, making great progress in their ability to speak their new language.

5. Keep the learning centers stocked with materials relevant to the vocabulary you are teaching. If you are studying animals of the northern US forest, the block area must have bears, deer, and wolves, not lions, tigers, and elephants. That attention to detail is not arbitrary. It is a purposeful way to build this new language.

6. Be explicit about the situations in which languages are used. For example, at home you speak English, at school you speak Spanish.

7. Declutter to make the environment easy to navigate. Clutter is stressful, and multilingual children have the heavier cognitive task of dealing with a language they are beginning to learn. If we ask a child to *find the scissors on the shelf in the art center*, the scissors should be easy to spot, not lost in the pencils area.

8. Sing with your own voices. Do not use recorded music from CDs or smart boards for singing. The tempo from recorded music is usually faster than the children can produce the sounds, and it becomes entertainment with little value for learning language. You may listen first, then turn it off and practice singing slowly at the children's pace.

9. Use technology with purpose. For example, you might show a short online video of counting in one of the languages in your classroom. Introduce the video: "Today we are going to watch a video about counting to ten in Korean. Na-Ri speaks Korean at home, so we will all hear what her language sounds like."

10. Alternate activities that require a lot of language with others that do not. Avoid having a long circle time when you read books and then sing songs afterward. Concentrate on the book and talk about it. Then go outside. Come back and have a second circle time with singing later.

CHAPTER 7: TEACHING THE SECOND LANGUAGE

At the beginning of the school year, when Albert wants to play with a toy truck, he puts his hand out with a big smile and says, "OK?" And more often than not he gets the truck he wants. Other children seek him out on the playground to run and laugh together. He is outgoing, an extrovert who interacts with everyone with gestures and one-word sentences. Marta spends most of her time at the art table, drawing and observing the room. She does not interact actively with other children, though she smiles quietly. When teachers approach, she looks up silently.

By February Albert has moved from one-word sentences to two or three words: "Me play," "More milk, please," "I like horse." But Marta's language production has not progressed. She is still quiet, and her teacher wonders whether she is learning. Both children are typically developing, and they are both learning to speak English but in different ways. Albert gets ongoing positive corrective feedback from the teachers, so he learns correct syntax and vocabulary that continue to expand his proficiency in English. Marta gets one-on-one and small-group tailored experiences so she can build her confidence one exchange at a time. By June assessments show that both children have made measurable progress with separate but equally rigorous approaches.

Considerations When Teaching a Second Language

Literacy is the ability to listen, speak, read, and write in any literate language. Early literacy is the preparation for literacy, and it starts with oral language. Some home languages do not have a written tradition. However, all children of the twenty-first century must become literate to succeed at home and at work. Early educators have the job to focus on the early literacy skills that young children need to know. These skills include

- phonological awareness—the knowledge of sounds in words, rhyming, alliteration;
- vocabulary—the words they know;
- oral language—the ability to use the words to say what they know, think, want, and feel;
- knowledge of the alphabet; and
- knowledge of books and print—understanding that books tell stories and share information (Collins and Schickedanz 2024).

To be ready to learn to read, children must have these foundational literacy skills. These are important for all languages, though the rules are different for each language. For example, considering phonological awareness, there are forty-four sounds in the English language. Specific sounds such as TH for Matthew, thunder, and thirsty requires practice for non-English speakers. To learn Mandarin in a Chinese immersion program, English-speaking children must practice the specific sounds of Mandarin repeatedly.

To become multilingual, children must know the sounds of the new language and then also understand vocabulary, including new words for objects, actions, and feelings. They must be able to communicate by using these new words with other children and adults in the appropriate way. For example, if Dani wants a turn at the cash register in the dramatic play store, she has to say, "I want to be the cashier." Or if Lucio misses his mom and his first reaction is to cry, he must understand the words his teacher says, "Your mommy will come back after naptime," and feel comforted.

Children approach the learning of a second language in individual ways. These differences relate to temperament, cognitive ability, sensory preferences, and motivation. Given the same amount of exposure, different children will have different results. Therefore, educators must differentiate their teaching techniques, as the teachers do in the vignette for Albert and Marta.

In the book *Raising a Bilingual Child*, researcher Barbara Zurer Pearson (2008) compares first and second language learning to learning to walk versus learning to ride a bicycle. Typically developing children learn to walk and talk in an organic way, through repeated practice supported by their environment. But learning to ride a bicycle takes extra steps, such as a tool (the bike), making specific movements (pedaling, maintaining equilibrium), and extra help and support from adults to master the skills.

Children who are learning a second language at school need intentional scaffolding. Just speaking to the children in the second language is not enough. The children may pick up some words, but they are not learning unless they get explicit instruction. For babies and toddlers, it means expanding their one-word or two-word utterances. For preschoolers who are using sentences, it means sometimes giving the language to articulate what they want to say. For example, a four-year-old child wants orange construction paper to make a pumpkin and points to it without words. The educator would scaffold his language learning by saying, "I want orange construction paper, please," and then, in a friendly tone, encourage the child to repeat it, affirming the child for using the sentence.

Educators and families must attend to the cognitive load of switching languages between home and school. For example, a child who attends a Spanish immersion program has to make that linguistic adjustment at drop-off and pickup time. It is more challenging for some children than for others, based on their temperament and their level of proficiency. To ease the transition, it is helpful to have quiet activity times such as sensory play that have low demand for language at both ends of the day.

Applying a Diversity and Equity Lens

The NAEYC position statement on Advancing Equity in Early Childhood Education (2019) recommends considering our own biases when teaching. Our biases can include assuming what children's linguistic and socio-cultural goals are without confirming the accuracy of our guesses. In multilingual classrooms, it is important to be aware of the tension between preserving home languages and acquiring English. In 2024 in the *Minneapolis Star Tribune*, Somali refugees said they did not come to the United States just to have kids learn their own culture and language: "We want them to be medical doctors. . . . We want them to be engineers. We want them to be lawyers and politicians" (Lonetree 2024). These families want their children to expand their linguistic and cultural horizons. Yet, in this example, in an effort to be sensitive, the school's curriculum tried to maintain the connection to the home culture by teaching about camels and desert life, while not being as rigorous in teaching English as the families wanted. Paying attention to equity involves listening to what families expect and responding accordingly, not following romantic notions or well-meaning opinions. Educators must be rigorous in teaching language in developmentally appropriate ways, whether it is English or another target language.

Practical Strategies for Teaching English or Another Second Language

1. Have linguistic goals that include a developmentally appropriate level of proficiency. For a toddler, it may be repeating common words like *drink*, *cat*, and *banana*. For a preschooler, it may be recognizing the words in a simple story like Bill Martin Jr.'s *Brown Bear, Brown Bear, What Do You See?* as well as using the words independently in conversation: "I see . . . a duck." Having goals helps educators focus on the vocabulary they need to teach.

2. Teach the language intentionally through explicit instruction that involves showing and telling children about an object or action. For example, if you are reading a book with the word *jump*, you would use a practice called front loading. This technique teaches the word before you encounter it in a story by saying the word *jump*, demonstrating how to jump, asking children to say the word, and encouraging them to jump with you. This ensures that the children have a good understanding of the word *jump* by the time they hear it in the story.

3. Have props and visual aids such as real objects or toy representations to teach vocabulary about objects, colors, size, and locations. Use a predictable routine: Show the object, say the word, ask the children to repeat with you, and point to the object in the illustration when reading the book.

4. Choose books with realistic illustrations and an interesting, dramatic story that can be acted out with gestures to catch the attention of the children. Both characteristics increase comprehension and make it easier for children to learn new words and concepts.

5. Read books using the technique of repeated read aloud by reading the same book several times a week (McGee and Schickedanz 2007).

6. While adults should not switch languages randomly, use translanguaging to boost children's growth in the second language. Children use their home language to process and augment their new language. If a child says, "My grandpa has a perro" (dog in Spanish), it is appropriate to expand "Your grandpa has a dog. A dog is a perro in English."

7. Use themes or projects for three or more weeks at a time. This gives children repeated opportunities to hear and practice new vocabulary words and concepts over many days and in many areas. If you are teaching vocabulary for the farm, think of how many times you can use just these three words: cow, dog, eat. Imagine how many opportunities there could be in dramatic play, at the painting easel, in storybooks, playing outdoors, in the gym, at the puzzle table, and so

on. Remember that you do not only want children to understand the words. You want them to say the words spontaneously and in context—that is the only way to become bilingual.

8. Engage in running commentary with parallel play, verbalizing what you are doing. For example, playing side by side at the playdough table, you may say, "I am rolling the dough, roll, roll, I roll the playdough."

9. Encourage the children to speak throughout the day, at mealtimes, dressing, brushing teeth, washing hands, indoors, and outdoors. Generally children are eager to learn and will repeat words or respond to communication. Even during the silent stage of second language development, educators should give frequent opportunities to practice producing the language. They can do that in a friendly manner. Give children words for sharing with a friend. You might say, for example, "Tell Pablo, I want a turn with the truck" or, on the playground, ask them, "Do you prefer the swing or the slide?"

10. Organize "pockets of play." These are small groups that you can organize formally during small-group time or during active learning time. You may choose children with similar proficiency levels so you can teach specific skills. Adults facilitate the play with specific vocabulary in mind, encouraging the children to share ideas with one another.

CHAPTER 8: HONORING HOME LANGUAGES

Ms. Sonya has a multilingual classroom of eighteen children. At home they speak English, Tamil, and Russian. Ms. Sonya does not speak Tamil or Russian, but she is committed to honoring the home languages in her group. She works with families and community members to find books in Tamil and Russian. She matches them to English books based on the topic of study. For example, if they are studying spring, she looks for books on the same theme, if not the same titles. She then enlists the help of volunteers to read to the children on a rotating basis every three weeks. In addition, Ms. Sonya has a regular schedule for using the home languages. She playfully greets the children and families every day in their home language, giving them the autonomy to respond in the language they chose. On Thursdays she has "international day" at circle time. Each week they alternate using Russian or Tamil, announced in this way: "Remember children, today is international day, and we are using Tamil today. So let's say good morning in Tamil. We will also sing in Tamil and listen to the story in Tamil too. Reka and Shoba speak Tamil at home, so they will understand the words. And we can all listen carefully to hear how it sounds." With this routine and other positive practices, all the children become aware of one another's languages, and a caring multilingual community is created.

Considerations for Honoring Home Languages

Both monolingual and multilingual early childhood educators can support home languages for all children to help them reach their full potential. They all show they value home languages with general skills and attitudes such as curiosity and empathy. Multilingual educators who know the home language of the children are a bonus in the classroom when they have a clear understanding of how and when to use the home language.

Honoring and supporting home languages must be intentional. It is not a matter of having someone who speaks the home language randomly using it. The use of home languages must be included in the lesson planning, so it is integrated into the overall instruction and daily routine.

The objective is to respect the home languages by giving them an official place in the curriculum. In addition to planned times such as book reading, greetings, songs, and games, it is important to talk about home languages in matter-of-fact conversations throughout the day, such as when children use their home language in play or when they make comments about their family life or the foods they eat at home.

When home languages become part of the curriculum, in addition to English, children develop metalinguistic awareness. That is, they learn that languages are tools that can be used to say words in different ways but with the same meaning. Multilingual learners demonstrate metalinguistic awareness when they can distinguish between languages. For example, Mohamed, a Somali-speaking child, will greet his friend José, a Spanish-speaking child, by laughing and shouting, "Buenos días," in Spanish. Then he says, "See, I speak Spanish too, like you!" As he and José giggle together, we know that they understand well that words in different languages convey ideas, and that language can even be used playfully.

Applying a Diversity and Equity Lens

The NAEYC position statement on Advancing Equity in Early Childhood Education (2019) recommends considering the developmental, cultural, and linguistic appropriateness of the learning environment and your teaching practices for each child. Honoring home languages is not teaching the language. It does not guarantee the maintenance of the home languages in the classroom. The definition of *honoring* is respecting and valuing. The opposite of honoring is ignoring. If we act as if the children do not have another language, we are leaving them behind. But when we honor all languages spoken in the classroom, children who speak another language at home feel included and respected. There is also a benefit for the children who speak only the target language. They learn that there are other languages besides their own, one that is spoken by their classmates and their families. Everyone in the classroom grows in their understanding of the richness of diversity.

Practical Strategies for Honoring Home Languages

1. Honor home languages to build relationships. As children and families hear their home language used respectfully and playfully, they feel like they belong in the space.

2. Learn from families, staff, and the community. Educators are not expected to know all the home languages, but they can learn some greetings, the correct pronunciation of names, and places of origin from native speakers.

3. Begin a routine of saying hello in home languages. Also use home languages formally for circle time greetings, songs, fingerplays, and book reading. As in the vignette, design a schedule that highlights classroom languages, and keep at it so that it becomes a routine that children anticipate.

4. Make the use of home languages predictable and explicit: "Today is Spanish day!" This could happen once a week or three times a week or once a month. It depends on the staff and volunteers you have. But it needs to be scheduled—it cannot be random.

5. Choose one or two songs related to a current theme or project in the home language. Schedule the songs on a day that language is being featured. If you are learning a song on a recording or video, listen to it once to get the tune and words, and then sing with your own voices.

6. Coordinate books in the home languages with your topic of study. Some books are available in many languages. It is worthwhile research to find books that are related by theme. For example, if your topic is spring, the objective might be to have the children realize that spring is *printemps* in French, *primavera* in Spanish, and *haru* in Japanese. Read the book in the home language to the entire classroom, even those who do not speak it. If you do not have a reader who speaks that language, you may find a video of the book being read online or find a community member to film or audio record themselves reading the book. You can introduce the reading by saying, "Today we are reading *The Very Hungry Caterpillar* in French. Marielle and Gaston speak French at home, and we want to hear what French sounds like. It is the same story we have read in English but different words. Let's all listen quietly now." This could be done once a week or once a month as your schedule allows.

7. Use a word wall to write key words in home languages next to English words. Ask families or staff who know the languages for the correct terminology.

8. Organize small groups of children who speak the same language for a special reading with an adult native speaker. This is most effective as a scheduled part of the lesson plan. Let the children know: "Today Ms. Marta is coming to read *The Very Hungry Caterpillar* in Spanish with Pedro, Mateo, and Carolina. You will go with Ms. Marta to the library center to read after lunch."

9. Inform families about the topic of study to let them know what the children are learning. Write a simple letter with six to twelve vocabulary words for the topic. Invite families to talk about the topic at home in their language so they can reinforce the concepts.

10. Schedule your multilingual staff or invite family or community members to your classroom to read a story or sing a song. It gives all children the chance to hear the language used by someone from outside their classroom.

CHAPTER 9: ASSESSMENT

Mateo is two years old and Lea is four years old. They speak Spanish at home. They are learning English in their child care center. Their pediatrician suggests that their language seems slow for their age. She refers them to the public school's early childhood assessment team for speech and language evaluation. With the family's permission, the early childhood assessment specialists observe the children in their classroom. They watch how they use language while playing with peers and how they interact verbally with adults. They find that Mateo mixes Spanish and English in one- to three-word sentences: "Quiero milk," "Give me camion." Lea appears calm in social interactions, but she does not say much in Spanish or English. The specialists talk with the parents, who say that Mateo mixes languages at home too, and that Lea is a chatterbox at home in Spanish. The assessment team feels that for now the children are on a good path but recommends that their teachers and parents continue observation. They also recommend concrete teaching strategies for the adults to follow. For Leo, they should provide gentle corrective feedback or extension. For example, when he says, "Quiero milk," the adults can encourage him to say, "I want milk." For Lea, educators should do a curriculum-based assessment for vocabulary to determine whether she is learning the words from the read alouds, and they should engage her in pockets of play with other children to facilitate her use of English with peers.

Considerations for Assessing Multilingual Learners

Multilingual toddlers are generally slower in productive language than monolinguals. Most families tend not to worry at this stage because they observe their children responding effectively in both languages and intuitively realize their total language is increasing.

However, this can cause concern for monolingual professionals in health care. After a well-child visit, a nurse or doctor may recommend the child undergo an assessment. This is to be taken seriously but not with alarm.

The best course is first to observe informally the children as they play and engage in classroom activities. How do they communicate nonverbally? What words do they use to say what they want, think, need, or feel? Do they repeat when prompted? Then educators should collaborate with families by asking their perception of their children's use of language. Finally, educators can conduct a more formal authentic assessment, considering the same questions as before and also documenting what happens and what the child does.

Authentic assessment is a process of learning the capabilities of a child thoughtfully and intentionally. The mark of authentic assessment is a continuous cycle of observing, planning instruction, and evaluating learning. (Some resources about performing authentic assessment include Bohart and Procopio [2018] and Alanís et al. [2021].) In the specific case of language learning, authentic assessment means watching the growth of productive language. The goal is not just noting that the child understands the meaning of a certain number of words but also documenting how they move beyond pointing and nonverbal expression to say what they want, need, feel, and know.

Children who are learning in more than one language may know some words in one language and other words in their other language. For example, they may know the words *cama* (bed), *lámpara* (lamp), and *regalo* (gift) in Spanish only, because these objects are part of the familiar vocabulary of home. And they may know the words *stapler*, *scissors*, and *brush* in English only, because these objects are part of the familiar vocabulary of the classroom. Put together, they know six words in two languages. This is called *additive vocabulary*. When assessing young children for language development, we must consider this additive vocabulary. And since they understand the concepts of these words, we must give them credit for the total knowledge they have.

Then educators must also ascertain whether the child is able to assign the correct word to the object in a given language. That gives the educator the clue to teach those words so the child learns them in the other language. For example, if the teacher points to the picture of a bed and the child says *cama*, the teacher can say, "Yes, it's *cama* in Spanish. And it's *bed* in English. *Cama* and *bed* are the same. Can you say *bed*?" With that short interaction, the teacher has assessed that the child has a concept of a *bed* and knows the word for *bed* in Spanish only at the moment. It tells the teacher that the child needs to learn the word for *bed* in English now.

Applying a Diversity and Equity Lens

The NAEYC position statement on Advancing Equity in Early Childhood Education (2019) recommends using authentic assessments to identify children's strengths and provide a well-rounded picture of their development and learning. That is particularly important for multilingual learners when it comes to language, as they are learning vocabulary in uneven ways, based on their daily experiences at home and at school.

The area of assessment is vulnerable to bias in both directions. Sometimes multilingual learners are overassessed: Educators or pediatricians worry early and do language assessments of toddlers, not considering the fact that they know as many words as monolingual toddlers when you consider their two languages, not just English. Other times children are underassessed, waiting to see if they will outgrow a seeming language deficit. Educators may want to give children the benefit of the doubt when they do not talk at school, attributing it to the silent period of second language development. At the same time, educators should complement their observations by talking with families. They can ask families for their own assessment of how the child is using their home language. Then educators can continue to observe and make more informed decisions about instruction or about possible referral for further evaluation.

Practical Strategies for Assessment of Multilingual Learners

1. Observe children carefully in your classroom. Start with a credible tool for observation like this one from the Centers for Disease Control and Prevention (CDC): www.cdc.gov/ncbddd/actearly/pdf/parents_pdfs/milestonemomentseng508.pdf. The format is easy to use with families too, as it describes children's expected behaviors in general, with a section for language development. Or use the tool provided by your program (such as Teaching Strategies GOLD).

2. Use authentic assessment strategies: Observe the children at play, document your observations by writing them down, reflect on what it means for teaching, use the analysis to adjust your teaching, and then repeat the process. To observe, you can also take a short video of children interacting and watch it later to take notes.

3. Assess first language development by collaborating with the family. Ask the family their view of the children's language at home: Do they say what they think, feel, know, and want in the home language (or in English)? This gives an indication of the child's communication and language development at home.

4. Assess second language development by designing your own curriculum-based assessment model. This can be done simply by choosing six to twelve words to teach with a read aloud (see chapter 6 for more details). Once a week, work with small groups of children and point out pictures, toys, or actions and ask them to say the words. For example, if you are reading "The Three Little Pigs" story, you would teach the words *pig, wolf, house, straw, sticks, brick, huff, puff,* and *blow.* Some of these words will be taught with objects, others with actions, and all with illustrations from the book. By the end of the week, you could expect the children to understand and say the words. If some vocabulary remains difficult, you know which words to continue to teach. This is also an opportunity to change the way you teach, using different demonstrations or examples.

5. Monitor each child's progress. As you record the words children are understanding and saying correctly, you will have a good picture of individual children's learning needs.

6. Continuous monitoring should happen frequently and in playful settings. In the example of "The Three Little Pigs" story, you assess for the words *brick, stick,* or *huff and puff* while children are on the playground or in the context of dramatic play.

7. Have a system for recording the information for each child. For example, plan to take notes on one-third of your group of children three days a week for fifteen minutes. The best time to record is during active learning, as you play with them. Some educators use a simple system of writing their observations on sticky notes and a clipboard.

8. Include examples of language learning in children's portfolios. You can include observational notes, quotes, audiotapes, or dictations to illustrate children's use of the target language and their home language. This is helpful data when assessing learning progress and for sharing with families and other professionals.

9. Be conscious of additive vocabulary. If a child uses their home language to name objects or situations or to respond to questions, take note that they have understood the concept but need more practice with the specific word in the target language.

10. Remember that children cannot learn what we don't teach them. This maxim is particularly important for vocabulary instruction. Use your observations and records to inform future instruction. When children are not responding correctly, ask yourself what could be done in your teaching. It might be more repetition, more clarity, or more opportunities to use the words in conversation and in play.

CHAPTER 10: BEHAVIOR GUIDANCE

Mason is enrolled in a Spanish immersion pre-K program. He speaks English at home, and his parents want him to learn Spanish so he gets the benefits of multilingualism. At story time, he puts his hands over his ears and screams, "No!" every few seconds. He is not the only one. Other children imitate Mason with variations. A temporary solution is for the teacher's aide to take Mason out for a walk in the hallway. But when he returns, he is upset again. These disruptive behaviors are annoying and worrisome for educators and parents. Their hope for his easy, seamless adaptation to a new language is not happening.

When an instructional coach comes to observe the situation, she notes that while some children passively listen even when they do not understand the story, others show signs that they need support. She suggests that the children get more scaffolding to manage story time in Spanish. Educators can remind children that the story is going to be in Spanish, a new language to their ears. It can help to use the preview-view-review technique: Give a summary of the story in English, read it in Spanish, then review the story summary in English. This technique works best when applied every day consistently. After a few days of this intentional routine, Mason begins to relax. First, he stops yelling. Then he uncovers his ears. He still has a frown, but he is listening. He is on his way to accepting this new language. Now he is more likely to reach his parents' goal of becoming multilingual. Without his disruptive behavior, the entire group dynamics improve. Story times are now manageable for the educators.

Considerations in Guiding the Behavior of Multilingual Learners

In language immersion child care programs, staff report easygoing times in the infant and young toddler rooms. The babies gurgle and smile contentedly. The toddlers begin to repeat foreign words: *agua*, *hola*, *yo*. Then life gets more challenging in the preschool rooms. The educators report increasing behavior problems, such as children who refuse to cooperate, who shout, "No!" like Mason, or who even try to escape the room.

Social-emotional development and language are closely tied. Children need to have the language to say what they feel, want, think, and know. When children are immersed in a language they do not understand, they feel as lost as a tourist on the back roads of a busy city, and so they express their anxieties in the best way they know how. Educators should not be surprised when they see behavior problems. But take heart: These challenges can be managed with some thoughtful strategies.

Educators who are otherwise attuned to characteristics of children such as sensory sensitivities or physical challenges often miss the cognitive challenges of learning a second language because they accept the myth of learning a second language as effortless. The reality is that learning a language puts a cognitive demand on multilingual learners, just like learning to play a musical instrument. It does require effort to understand new words and to say them, even when children are familiar with the concepts. The simple announcement of the teacher before reading at story time sounds very different in English ("Let's read the story now") and Spanish ("Ahora, vamos a leer este cuento"). Children have to understand what the teacher is saying first. Then they have to adjust their behavior to comply with the expectations of listening quietly to a story with words they do not fully grasp.

Once children are nearing fluency, language becomes an internalized tool for regulating thoughts and actions: "I want this truck. But Tomi has it already. I am going to ask him if we can share." This complex processing of thoughts and actions is developmental, easier for six-year-olds than for two-year-olds. Now, just imagine doing it in a foreign language, even if you are six and have already progressed from physical to verbal problem solving in your home language!

When the cognitive task becomes too much work, it turns into a cognitive challenge. And faced with this challenge, some children react negatively and act up like Mason.

Despite the common hope of many adults, learning another language is a cognitive demand that is onerous for children, for some more than others. These children do adapt, but they need extra support. They need scaffolding to alleviate the difficulty of understanding the new words they are hearing. Educators must be intentional in smoothing the way to learn the new language, with strategies that make the environment predictable, help children process the successes and challenges of being multilingual, and explicitly teach vocabulary for social-emotional skills. In that way, educators address the children's cognitive, social, and emotional development.

Applying a Diversity and Equity Lens

The NAEYC position statement on Advancing Equity in Early Childhood Education (2019) encourages educators to consider how their biases influence their interactions with children and the messages they send. The advice applies here to the act of learning languages. If we believe that learning a language is simple, we may ignore the signals children send us through challenging behavior. We focus on fixing the behavior rather than attending to the symptom, the cognitive load of language learning. In an equitable environment, educators consider the role of language learning in behavior and apply strategies that prevent negative reactions and that help children cope—in addition to teaching them the target language.

Practical Strategies for Behavior Guidance

1. Acknowledge to children that learning another language is hard work. This validates the experience for them. Let them know they are learning actively, just the way you would congratulate them for a physical act of learning to ride a tricycle or finishing a puzzle. The message is "You are working hard and you can learn this!"

2. Remind children frequently that they are learning a new language different from their home language: "In our classroom, we are learning to speak in Mandarin. Mandarin sounds different from English, doesn't it?" Talking about language learning explicitly honors children's experience.

3. Organize the day with routines to create a predictable pattern that frees children from having to figure out what is happening. Knowing the sequence of the day is reassuring. Children learn that they can expect that circle time comes after breakfast, and outdoor time after that, and then story time, and so on.

4. Write and post a visual schedule to show children the sequence of activities. When multilingual children miss verbal cues, they benefit from visual cues to recognize their environment and trust its logic. Show it and talk about the visual schedule at formal times such as circle. Refer to it throughout the day to remind children of what comes next. For example, right before cleanup, you might say, "It's time to finish playing in five minutes. It will be cleanup time. See on the chart." The goal is

to minimize surprises that create discomfort, which often shows up as challenging behaviors in young children.

5. Have quiet spaces to lower the cognitive load and provide safe havens away from the overstimulation of listening and speaking a new language. It may be the library center with soft toys and simple board books or a small tent in the corner of the room.

6. Alternate activities to avoid overload of language-rich activities, such as singing and reading a story back-to-back at circle time. Two short circle times are better than one long one.

7. Use small groups to distribute children by language ability. Sometimes groups with mixed abilities allow children to learn from one another. Other times it is helpful to have children with similar proficiency (high or low) together with an adult who facilitates conversation so everyone has a chance to talk on a more even level.

8. Use running commentary to promote friendships among children who do not have a common language. This can happen in all centers of the room or at any time of the day. At the puzzle table, you may comment, "Theo and Mason, you are both working on puzzles," or in the dramatic play center, you may say, "Maria and Sonya, you are making soup together for the babies." Smiling adults noticing positive play encourage both language development and social-emotional development.

9. Use techniques that use movement to augment comprehension in playful ways. For example, Total Physical Response (TPR) engages children with their whole body to perform needed tasks in the classroom. It is akin to games like Simon Says, where you show an action that fits the situation. As you say, "It's story time now," show the book in your hand, march the children to the rug, and show them how to sit at the same time. These actions promote a sense of camaraderie, working together in a fun manner.

10. Teach explicitly the words children need to say what they feel, want, think, and know. It can be with TPR, demonstrating "I am happy" or "I am angry" as part of a vocabulary lesson while reading a story. Or it can be organic as you observe tension rising over the sharing of a toy. Help children say the words "I want a turn with the red truck." Then stay with them as they resolve the issue. Finally, congratulate them on the successful resolution, emphasizing the language part: "Mason and José, you are learning the Spanish words for taking turns when you play!"

CONCLUSION: A MULTILINGUAL, MULTICULTURAL PLANET

> Language is more than a tool for communication; it's a very specific human cognitive faculty and the foundation of our shared humanity. It enables the transmission of experiences, traditions, knowledge and identities across generations.
>
> Languages play a crucial role in promoting peace, fostering intercultural dialogue, and driving sustainable development. They permeate every facet of our lives—from family and work to education, politics, media, justice, research and technology. Our values, beliefs, knowledge, identities and worldviews are intricately shaped by language, reflecting the richness of the human experience.
> (Giannini 2024)

On the internet and in daily conversations, I hear a romantic version of multilingualism. That it is wonderful. That the world can only benefit. That it is easy, since children are like sponges and absorb languages effortlessly. As a literate trilingual myself, I agree it is wonderful to know more than one language. I do disagree with the sponge theory of learning. Children learning a second language are active learners, and they work hard at it. They need a rigorous curriculum with academic linguistic goals and socio-cultural goals. I hope I have given you this understanding and that you have gathered useful tips for teaching multilingual learners.

And as I end this book, I also want to offer thoughts on multicultural education from a world perspective. That may seem a bit too far away and irrelevant to our day-to-day work with children in your classroom. But I believe it is important because we should have a broader view as we ask ourselves why we teach multilingual children in our classroom. We should be aware of the impact on the future of our planet.

Multilingualism is on the global agenda as the influence of artificial intelligence and the internet spreads rapidly. The world appears to be moving toward common languages to streamline communication. According to the United Nations Educational, Scientific and Cultural Organization (UNESCO), there are about seven thousand languages spoken in the world, with just a few of them written (Giannini 2024). Many languages are dialects without a literate tradition, so they are at risk of disappearing.

As global social and economic movements on our planet rush ahead, governments are attempting to adapt their education systems to teach their children at least one global language in addition to the country's main dialect. In nations with literate languages, multilingualism is a matter of applying sound rules of teaching so children can become literate in both their home language and another language. Children in Germany or Spain can learn to speak, read, and write in German and Spanish, and in English. Since the nineteenth century, these countries have had standard languages for education and official communication, even if dialects are spoken in local communities.

Yet in many places, even identifying a country's main dialect can be complicated. Many nations of Africa, Asia, and Latin America have a big web of local and indigenous oral languages that are used. For example, in the Philippines more than 180 dialects or languages are spoken among 2,000 inhabited islands, so people cannot easily communicate with one another. Therefore, the government has mandated two official languages to streamline communication: Filipino and English. English is often chosen as the second language. Likewise around the world, many governments are trying to unify the citizenry by instituting an official literate language. They do so through the educational system. That means that many children do not use their home languages to learn at school. They learn to read in the literate language of instruction but do not use their home language in their formal education. These home languages have vocabulary for informal social interactions and customs, but they do not have the vocabulary for philosophical, literary, mathematical, and scientific thinking that are needed to participate in the economic and political international stage.

Some adaptations are plainly utilitarian. For example, the International Civil Aviation Organization (ICAO) mandates English as the common language for pilots and air traffic controllers. Without a standardized system for communication, safe air travel would be impossible. *Up*, a simple little word I imagine frequently used in the field, sounds like this in different tongues: *arriba* (Spanish), *en haut* (French), *aelaa* (Arabic), *su* (Italian), and *hoch* (German). None of it is intuitive! So streamlining language for the future in aviation as well as in medicine and computers does seem necessary. Indeed, we must take a pragmatic approach toward multilingualism.

This reality points to the urgency of honoring home languages even if they do not match the complexity of literate languages and are not practical for science and technology. In addition to teaching the "window" of a new language for educational attainment and better professional chances, educators must pay much attention to the "mirror" of home languages so children feel accepted and respected. The preservation of home languages is important for the "transmission of experiences, traditions, knowledge and identities across generations" (Giannini 2024). This principle should apply to the education of children everywhere.

As educators teach their little multilingual learners, they cannot guarantee the survival of every language, but they can commit to respecting and valuing all the languages they encounter in their classrooms, be it Ojibwe, African American English, Spanish, Mandarin, Haitian Creole, or Quichua. In that way they contribute positively to the best of both worlds: a common language for global communication and a home language for family communication. The children benefit from learning the language of power to succeed in school and work. And they benefit from the respect given to their heritage language.

Families want the best for their children. Immigrant and refugee families are clear that they have left their home country seeking better opportunities for their children, especially a chance at a good education. If you teach in a program with immigrant and refugee children, you must teach them the best English that you can while you purposefully honor their home language with the techniques described in this book. English-speaking families want to give their children opportunities to enhance their knowledge. If you teach in a language immersion program, you have the job of teaching the children to think, talk, read, and write in the second language. But you also must honor their English language. Even if it is dominant, it should not be casually ignored. It is still part of the development of the babies, toddlers, and preschoolers that you care for during a large part of the day. They need the reassurance of having their home language acknowledged in your classroom too.

A successful multilingual program is a vibrant community of people sharing life, language, and learning. By teaching English or another immersion language every day, you are giving the children the skill of a new language to succeed at school and at work. By intentionally scheduling support for all the home languages in your setting, you formally recognize children's cultures and show that you value them and their families.

I hope you will add the recommendations from this book to your daily teaching practices in your multilingual program. It is a big responsibility. And it is also an exciting journey. You are transforming children's lives by introducing them to a new language. By extension you are also introducing them to a new culture. I wish you the very best as you continue your good work.

CHECKLIST

This checklist is intended as an overview for teaching multilingual learners, organized around each book chapter. It is a tool for self-assessment and planning. All the items are important. When completed, it serves as an action plan. You can use it to focus on the items that are low. Then you can take the steps described in the chapters to improve quality for multilingual learners. Check the appropriate box on a scale of 1 (lowest) to 3 (highest).

In our program we:	1 rarely	2 sometimes	3 frequently
First and Second Language Development			
Understand and can explain first language development			
Understand and can explain second language development			
Show enthusiasm for language and words in books			
Use translanguaging as intentional pedagogy			
Give positive feedback so children know they are communicating successfully			
Planning Program			
Set socio-cultural goals for the children			
Set linguistic goals for the children			
Adapt the curriculum to meet the goals			

Invest in professional development of staff			
Understand and budget the added cost of teaching multilingual learners			
Working with Families			
Explain to families the process of second language learning and multilingualism			
Explain the role of second language in academic success			
Teach families how to maintain home language at home			
Before a curriculum unit begins, share key vocabulary and concepts with families in English and home language so they can reinforce the learning of language at home			
Teach families how to reinforce the second language learning at home			
Supporting Monolingual Educators			
Help educators process concerns and questions			
Provide resources in response to concerns			
Provide group professional development or individual coaching on teaching English			
Provide group professional development or individual coaching on honoring English			
Support educators' integration into a caring community of multilingual, multicultural workers			
Supporting Multilingual Educators			
Help educators process concerns and questions			
Provide resources in response to concerns			

Provide group professional development or individual coaching for the educational use of home languages and English to teach children			
Provide group professional development or individual coaching on English oral and writing skills			
Support staff integration into a caring community of multi-lingual, multicultural workers			
Use English as the professional language for the program, with use of translanguaging to increase comprehension			
Focus on Early Literacy in the Environment, Curriculum, and Materials			
Keep the environment uncluttered			
Conduct repeated read alouds to reinforce vocabulary			
Choose materials related to the focus vocabulary			
Hold topics of study for three weeks or more to promote repetition and exposure to key vocabulary			
Teaching the Second Language			
Have linguistic goals that include age-appropriate levels of proficiency			
Teach vocabulary through explicit instruction with actions, props, and visual aids			
Read books with realistic illustrations and interesting stories			
Respect the children's ability to use their first language to build their second language			
Encourage the children to speak throughout the day and the activities			
Organize pockets of play to facilitate conversation among children			

Honoring Home Languages			
Openly acknowledge and celebrate all home languages in the classroom or program			
Have predictable routines to honor home languages			
Learn about languages from families, staff, and the community			
Coordinate books and curriculum activities in English and home languages			
Invite home language speakers to read or play with children on a predictable schedule			
Assessment			
Assess first (home) language learning in collaboration with family			
Assess second language learning in the classroom with curriculum-based assessment (related to the vocabulary taught in the unit)			
Use authentic assessment methods: observe during play and normal course of day and record observations			
Adjust instruction based on the assessment			
Behavior Guidance			
Understand that some challenging behaviors may be related to a child's struggle to learn a second language			
Have consistent predictable routines so children can anticipate activities			
Use scaffolding techniques such as TPR, Simon Says, or follow-the-leader games, to make it easier for children to follow routines and understand directions			

Provide quiet spaces for respite from intensity of hearing a second language			
Acknowledge and celebrate the cognitive effort of children learning a new language			
A Multilingual, Multicultural Planet			
Recognize that multilingualism and multiculturalism are related			
Recognize the value of English for global communication			
Recognize the value of home languages for community and family communication			
Work toward biliteracy (or multiliteracy): the ability to listen, talk, and read or write in two or more languages			
Celebrate the multilingual, multicultural nature of our classroom or program			

RESOURCES

Centers for Disease Control and Prevention Developmental Milestones

www.cdc.gov/ncbddd/actearly/milestones/index.html

The milestones and parent tips give simple and accurate information on all aspects of development. This resource is useful for parents and educators and is published in multiple languages.

Colorín Colorado

www.colorincolorado.org

This bilingual website (in English and Spanish) is for families and educators of multilingual learners. The strategies they describe can be generalized to languages other than Spanish.

Enterprise League

https://enterpriseleague.com/blog/breaking-down-language-barriers

This webpage on the Enterprise League's website focuses on multilingual workplaces. Though not focused on early childhood education, the articles and advice apply to multilingual teams in any industry.

Head Start | Culture and Language

https://headstart.gov/culture-language

This website has an extensive library of information on teaching multilingual learners and supporting their families.

Milet Publishing

www.milet.com

Milet is a multilingual publisher that has titles in twenty-six languages, including picture dictionaries.

Multilingual Learning Toolkit

www.multilinguallearningtoolkit.org

The Multilingual Learning Toolkit offers resources on instructional practices to educators who support multilingual learners in pre-K to third grade.

National Association for the Education of Young Children (NAEYC)

www.naeyc.org/resources/topics/dual-language-learners

NAEYC is a member organization for early childhood educators. In addition to sponsoring national and state conferences, it has an extensive library of books, articles, and resources for teaching multilingual learners.

NIEER: National Institute for Early Education Research

https://nieer.org/self-evaluation-supports-emergent-bilingual-acquisition-seseba

NIEER offers research-based assistance and professional development. It has designed Supporting English and Spanish Emergent Bilingual Acquisition (SESEBA), a tool to support educators working with multilingual learners.

Reading Rockets

www.readingrockets.org

Reading Rockets offers information and resources on how young kids learn to read. It has an extensive section on multilingual learners.

UNESCO (United Nations Educational, Scientific and Cultural Organization)

www.unesco.org/en/articles/multilingual-education-key-quality-and-inclusive-learning

The UNESCO website offers a worldwide perspective on multilingual learning.

REFERENCES

Alanís, Iliana, Irasema Salinas-González, and María G. Arreguín. 2021. *The Essentials: Dual Language Learners in Diverse Environments in Preschool and Kindergarten.* NAEYC.

Baker, Colin, and Wayne E. Wright. 2021. *Foundations of Bilingual Education and Bilingualism.* Multilingual Matters.

Bialystok, Ellen. 2001. *Bilingualism in Development: Language, Literacy, and Cognition.* Cambridge University Press.

Bohart, Holly, and Rossella Procopio, eds. 2018. *Spotlight on Young Children: Observation and Assessment.* NAEYC.

Bruner, Jerome. 1983. *Child's Talk: Learning to Use Language.* Norton.

Buysse, V., D. C. Castro, and E. Peisner-Feinberg. 2010. "Effects of a Professional Development Program on Classroom Practices and Outcomes for Latino Dual Language Learners." *Early Childhood Research Quarterly* 25 (2): 194–206.

Castro, Dina C., Eugene E. García, and Amy M. Markos. 2013. "Dual Language Learners: Research Informing Policy." The University of North Carolina, Frank Porter Graham Child Development Institute, Center for Early Care and Education—Dual Language Learners. https://fpg.unc.edu/sites/fpg.unc.edu/files/resources/reports-and-policy-briefs/FPG_CECER-DLL_ResearchInformingPolicyPaper.pdf.

Chomsky, Noam. 1965. *Aspects of the Theory of Syntax.* MIT Press.

Collins, Molly F., and Judith A. Schickedanz. 2024. *So Much More than the ABCs: The Early Phases of Reading and Writing.* Rev. ed. NAEYC.

Cummins, Jim. 1979. "Cognitive/Academic Language Proficiency, Linguistic Interdependence, the Optimum Age Question and Some Other Matters." Working Papers on Bilingualism, No. 19. https://eric.ed.gov/?id=ED184334.

Genesee, Fred. 2016. "North America: Rethinking Early Childhood Education for English Language Learners: The Role of Language." In *Early Childhood Education in English for Speakers of Other Languages*, edited by Victoria. A. Murphy and Maria Evangelou. British Council.

Giannini, Stefania. 2024. "Multilingual Education: A Key to Quality and Inclusive Learning." *UN Chronicle*, February 20. www.un.org/en/un-chronicle/multilingual-education-key-quality-and-inclusive-learning.

Goldenberg, C. 2008. *Teaching English Language Learners: What the Research Does—and Does Not—Say*. American Educator.

Lonetree, Anthony. 2024. "A St. Paul School Was in Trouble but Its Principal Turned It Around by Listening to Parents. *Minneapolis Star Tribune*, May 12. www.startribune.com/a-st-paul-school-was-in-trouble-its-principal-turned-it-around-by-listening-to-parents/600365367.

Masterson, Marie. 2022. "Planning and Implementing an Engaging Curriculum to Achieve Meaningful Goals." In *Developmentally Appropriate Practice in Early Childhood Programs Serving Children from Birth Through Age 8*, edited by NAEYC. 4th ed. NAEYC.

McGee, Lea M., and Judith A. Schickedanz. 2007. "Repeated Interactive Read-Alouds in Preschool and Kindergarten. *The Reading Teacher* 60 (8): 742–51.

NAEYC (National Association for the Education of Young Children). 2019. "Advancing Equity in Early Childhood Education." Position statement. NAEYC. www.naeyc.org/resources/position-statements/equity.

———. 2022. *Developmentally Appropriate Practice in Early Childhood Programs Serving Children from Birth Through Age 8*, edited by NAEYC. 4th ed. NAEYC.

Paschall, Katherine, Rebecca Madill, and Tamara Halle. 2020. Demographic Characteristics of the Early Care and Education Workforce: Comparisons with Child and Community Characteristics. OPRE Report #2020-108. Office of Planning, Research, and Evaluation, Administration for Children and Families, US Department of Health and Human Services. https://acf.gov/sites/default/files/documents/opre/demographic-characteristics-ECE-dec-2020.pdf.

Passe, Angèle Sancho. 2013. *Dual-Language Learners, Birth to Age 8: Strategies for Teaching English*. Redleaf Press.

———. 2015. *Evaluating and Supporting Early Childhood Teachers*. Redleaf Press.

Pearson, Barbara Zurer. 2008. *Raising a Bilingual Child: A Step-by-Step Guide for Parents*. Living Language, Random House.

Sims Bishop, R. 1990. "Mirrors, Windows, and Sliding Glass Doors." In *Collected Perspectives: Choosing and Using Books for the Classroom*, edited by Hughes Moir. Christopher-Gordon Publishers.

Tabors, Patton O. 2008. *One Child, Two Languages: A Guide for Early Childhood Educators of Children Learning English as a Second Language*. 2nd ed. Brookes Publishing Company.

Wasik, Barbara A., and Annemarie H. Hindman. 2011. "Improving Vocabulary and Pre-Literacy Skills of At-Risk Preschoolers Through Teacher Professional Development." *Journal of Educational Psychology* 103 (2): 455–69. https://doi.org/10.1037/a0023067.

Williams, Connor. 2017. "The Intrusion of White Families into Bilingual Schools" *The Atlantic Monthly*. December 28. www.theatlantic.com/education/archive/2017/12/the-middle-class-takeover-of-bilingual-schools/549278.

Zelasko, Nancy, and Beth Antunez. 2000. *If Your Child Learns Two Languages: A Parent's Guide for Improving Educational Opportunities for Children Acquiring English as a Second Language*. National Clearinghouse for Bilingual Education. https://eric.ed.gov/?id=ED447713.